mushrooms and molds

mushrooms and molds

BY ROBERT FROMAN

Illustrated by Grambs Miller

Thomas Y. Crowell Company, New York

LET'S-READ-AND-FIND-OUT SCIENCE BOOKS

Editors: *DR. ROMA GANS*, Professor Emeritus of Childhood Education, Teachers College, Columbia University

DR. FRANKLYN M. BRANLEY, Chairman and Astronomer of The American Museum–Hayden Planetarium

Air Is All Around You
Animals in Winter
A Baby Starts to Grow
Bats in the Dark
Bees and Beelines
Before You Were a Baby
The Beginning of the Earth
The Big Dipper
Big Tracks, Little Tracks
Birds at Night
Birds Eat and Eat and Eat
Bird Talk
The Blue Whale
The Bottom of the Sea
The Clean Brook
Cockroaches:
   Here, There, and Everywhere
Down Come the Leaves
A Drop of Blood
Ducks Don't Get Wet
The Emperor Penguins
Find Out by Touching
Fireflies in the Night
Flash, Crash, Rumble, and Roll
Floating and Sinking
Follow Your Nose
Fossils Tell of Long Ago
Giraffes at Home

Glaciers
Gravity Is a Mystery
Green Turtle Mysteries
Hear Your Heart
High Sounds, Low Sounds
Hot as an Ice Cube
How a Seed Grows
How Many Teeth?
How You Talk
Hummingbirds in the Garden
Icebergs
In the Night
It's Nesting Time
Ladybug, Ladybug, Fly
   Away Home
The Listening Walk
Look at Your Eyes*
A Map Is a Picture
The Moon Seems to Change
Mushrooms and Molds
My Daddy Longlegs
My Five Senses
My Hands
My Visit to the Dinosaurs
North, South, East, and West
Oxygen Keeps You Alive
Rain and Hail
Rockets and Satellites

Salt
Sandpipers
Seeds by Wind and Water
Shrimps
The Skeleton Inside You
Snow Is Falling
Spider Silk
Starfish
Straight Hair, Curly Hair*
The Sun: Our Nearest Star
The Sunlit Sea
A Tree Is a Plant
Upstairs and Downstairs
Use Your Brain
Watch Honeybees with Me
Water for Dinosaurs and You
Weight and Weightlessness
What Happens to a Hamburger
What I Like About Toads
What Makes a Shadow?
What Makes Day and Night
What the Moon Is Like*
Where Does Your Garden Grow?
Where the Brook Begins
Why Frogs Are Wet
The Wonder of Stones
Your Skin and Mine*

* AVAILABLE IN SPANISH

L.C. Card 71-187936

ISBN 0-690-56602-6
    0-690-56603-4 (LB)

1   2   3   4   5   6   7   8   9   10

mushrooms and molds

LET'S READ AND FIND OUT →

One day the ground may be covered with grass or
weeds.
But there is no sign of mushrooms.

The next day—there are mushrooms.
Sometimes just one or two.

Sometimes dozens of them.

A mushroom is a fungus.

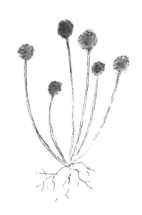

A mold is a fungus, too.

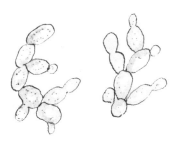

So are yeasts and puffballs and several other kinds
   of plants.
Sometimes all of them together are called funguses,
   but more often they are called fungi.

Fungi are plants, but they are very different from
   other plants.
The leaves of trees and grasses and flowers and weeds
   are natural food factories.
These green leaves mix air and water with minerals
   from the ground.
With the help of sunlight they turn them into food
   which helps the plants grow.
Some may grow fast; others take a long time.

Fungi cannot make their own food.

They must get their food from other plants or from animals.

People used to think that magic made mushrooms suddenly pop up out of the ground.

Mushrooms seem to pop up out of nowhere because they grow out of a tangle of fibers that grow underground.

These tangled fibers do not look anything like mushrooms.

They look like messy spider webs.

Such a tangle is called a mycelium.

It is hard to find because its parts are very thin — as thin as threads. They grow every which way. Because they grow underground, they are hard to see.

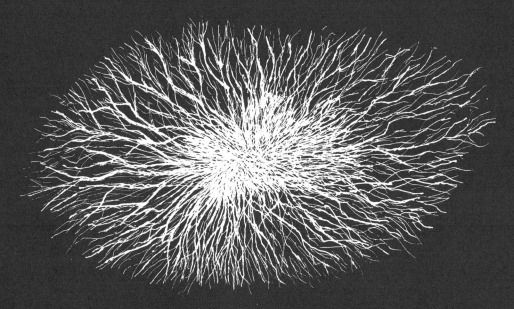

MYCELIUM

You can grow one kind of mycelium out in the open
   where it is easy to see.
You can grow a mold mycelium on a piece of bread.
Put a small piece of bread on a saucer. Sprinkle a
   little water on it.
Rub your finger on the floor to pick up a little dust.
Then rub your finger across the bread.
Cover the bread with a cup or bowl and put it in a
   warm place.

Wait for two or three days, then look at the bread.

If the bread is dry and there is nothing growing on it, put a little more water on it.

After a while you will find little spots of white, dark brown, or other colors on the bread.

These spots are mold plants.

They will grow bigger and bigger if you keep the bread warm and moist.

With a magnifying glass you can see that each plant is a tangle of threads going in all directions. It is a mycelium.

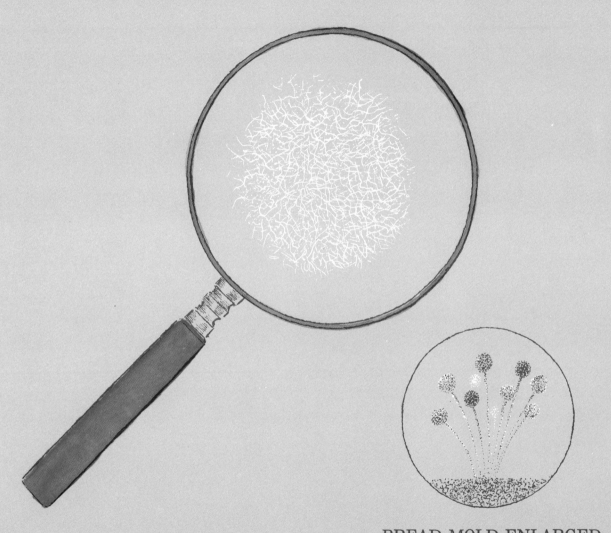

BREAD MOLD ENLARGED

13

As the molds grow on your piece of bread, they will change the bread into a kind of paste.
Green plants could use the minerals in this paste as food.

Fungi change dead plants and animals they grow on
into food for green plants.

When the mycelium grows under the ground, it
changes dead leaves and bits of wood into plant
food.

Some mushrooms and other fungi don't grow out of
  the ground.
They grow on the sides of trees or on dead stumps
  and logs.

They help turn the wood to soil for grasses and bushes and new trees and other plants to grow in. All the different kinds of fungi help to turn wood and leaves and dead animals into soil.

Where do all these fungi come from—the yeasts, mushrooms, and molds?

Not from seeds.

Inside the seed of a green plant there is a tiny plant ready to grow.

And there is a supply of food to help it get started.

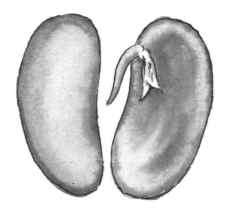

BEAN SEED

19

Mushrooms and molds and other fungi do not make
  seeds.
Instead they make spores.
A fungus spore is a tiny plant.
But a spore contains only a tiny bit of food.
It can start growing only if it falls on a place where
  there is exactly the food it needs.

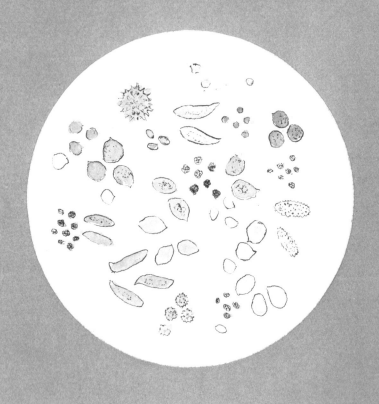

Sometimes only one spore in a million — or one spore
in hundreds of millions — falls on a place where it
can grow.
But a single fungus sends out millions and millions
of spores.

The spores are so light that they float in the air.

Did you ever see a ray of sunlight with lots of tiny specks of dust floating in it?

Many of those specks are fungus spores.

That is why molds grew from the dust you put on the bread.

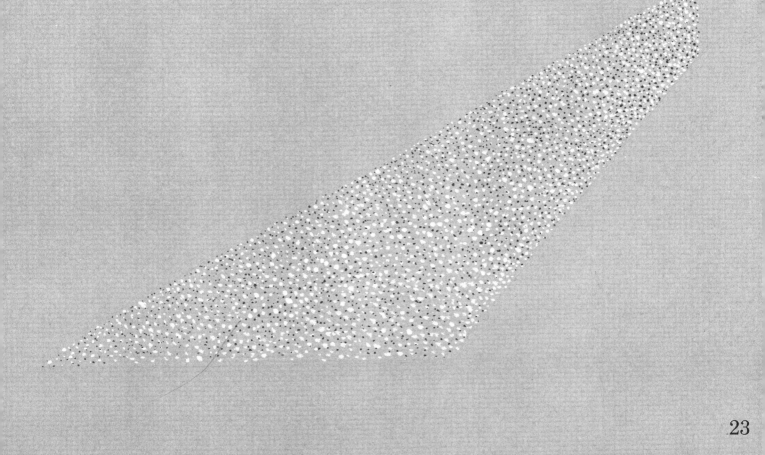

When you look at bread molds with a magnifying glass, you can see threads growing every which way.

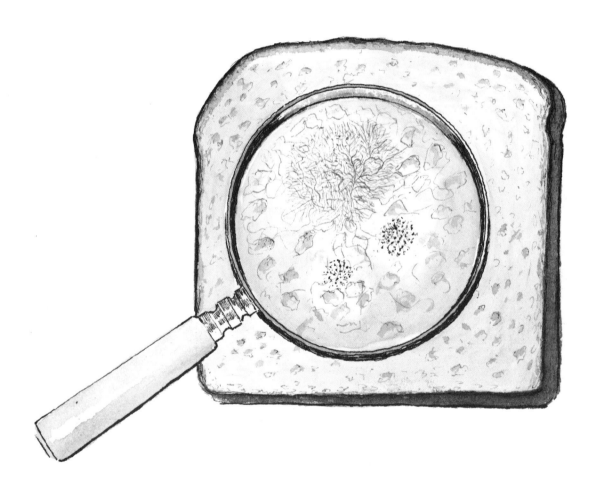

If you look very closely, you can also see little bumps
here and there on the threads.
These bumps are where the molds make spores.

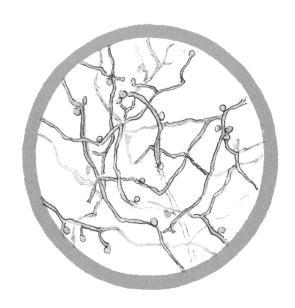

VERY ENLARGED

Mushrooms are really big bumps on the mushroom mycelium.

They are where mushroom spores are made.

The underground mycelium sends up mushrooms when it is time to make spores.

Many mushrooms have caps.

The spores grow on gills inside the caps.

When the spores are ripe they fall.

They are so tiny that you can't see one of them alone.

But when hundreds of them are together, you can see them.

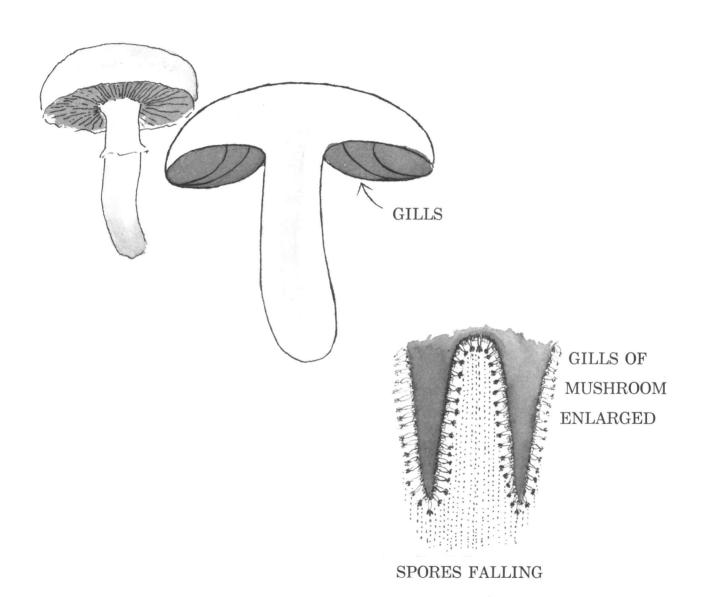

GILLS

GILLS OF
MUSHROOM
ENLARGED

SPORES FALLING

Here is a way to see mushroom spores.

Break the stem off a fresh mushroom.

Put the cap flat on a piece of paper.

Cover the cap with a glass and leave it overnight.

The spores will fall on the paper in a pattern.

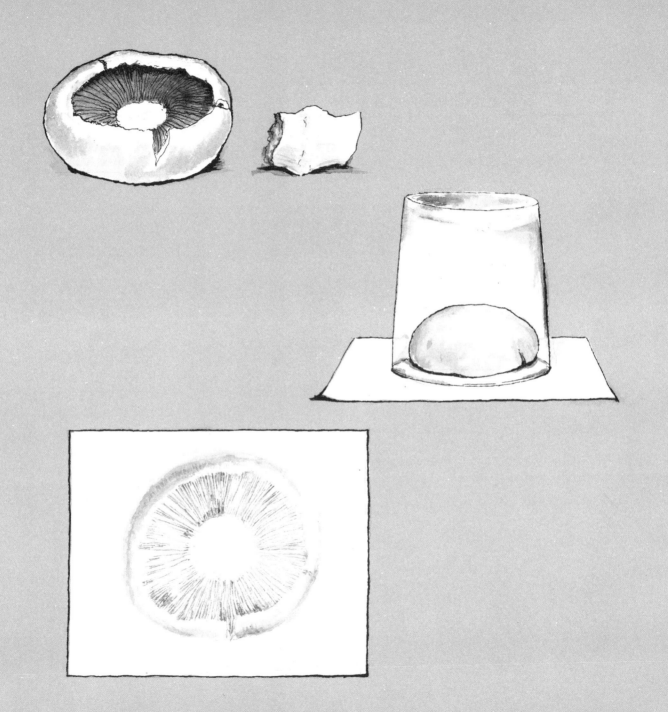

Different kinds of mushrooms have different-colored
spores.
They fall in different patterns.

31

When you blow on the paper, the spores disappear.
They may float out the window or door or up a chimney.
They may float on and on for miles.
The spores that fall in the right places will grow into fungi.
They will help make soil on which other living things can grow.

33

ABOUT THE AUTHOR

Robert Froman decided when he was about eleven that he wanted to be a writer, and he has never had any other occupation. He is now author of more than twenty books and some two hundred articles. Most of his writing has been on scientific subjects, and he says that he particularly enjoys introducing young readers to the "delight of learning."

Mr. Froman was born in Big Timber, Montana, and educated in Idaho and Oregon. With his wife, Elizabeth Hull Froman, who is also an author of children's books, he now lives in Tomkins Cove, New York.

ABOUT THE ARTIST

Grambs Miller was born in Peking, China, and lived there until she was seventeen. Exhibitions of her drawings in Peking, Hong Kong, and Shanghai won her a scholarship to the Art Students League in New York, where she studied with George Grosz, Thomas Hart Benton, and John Steuart Curry.

Mrs. Miller has illustrated many books, on subjects ranging from roses to Chinese cooking. With her husband she lives in New York City and summers on Martha's Vineyard, where she is an enthusiastic observer of nature.